Easy All-Natural Cooking

Fish & Seafood and Vegetarian Cookbook

Introduction

All-natural cooking is much easier than it sounds. Mother Nature provides us with the healthiest, freshest ingredients that we can creatively combine in order to make some truly memorable meals. Modern-day convenience dictates that we should buy premade dinners and heat them up in order to save time. What if we told you that cooking naturally is not time-consuming at all? This collection of 40 amazing fish and seafood recipes will make you the all-star as you serve your family a healthy, delicious dinner or lunch in minutes!

Table of Contents

New England Clam Chowder

Calamari with Ginger Sauce

Thai Steamed Mussels

Chinese Mustard Baked Salmon

Baked Tilapia Filets

Fresh Sashimi Bento Bowl

Fresh Clams with Cocktail Sauce

Asian Shrimp Lettuce Wraps

Smoked Salmon Avocado Salad

Tuna Tartar with Avocado and Mango

City Clam Chowder

Salmon Tartar Stack

Garlic and White Wine Steamed Mussels

Shrimp Stuffed Squid

Lobster Newburg

Seafood Paella

Easy Tuna Tartar Crêpes

Smoked Salmon Eggs Benedict

All-Natural Seared Tuna Salad

Tilapia Ceviche

Oyster Po' Boy

Long Rolls

Tuna Sandwich

Sandwich Bread

Healthy Shrimp Taco

Grain-Free Tortillas

Coconut Shrimp

Clams Casino

Crispy Soft Shell Crab With Garlic Lemon Aioli

Almond Crusted Pan Seared Scallops

Basque Style Cod Fish Stew

All-Natural Lobster Bisque

Red Snapper Soup

New England Clam Chowder

Prep Time: 10 minutes

Cook Time: 40 minutes

Servings: 4

INGREDIENTS

24 - 36 medium live littleneck clams (or other clam varieties)

2 cans (14 oz) full-fat coconut milk

3 - 4 cups clam juice (or fish stock or chicken stock)

4 slices nitrate-free bacon

4 medium parsnips

1 small onion

1 garlic clove

1 tablespoon tapioca flour (or arrow root powder)

1 1/2 teaspoons ground white black pepper (or black pepper)

1 teaspoon Celtic sea salt

Small bunch fresh parsley (for garnish)

Water

INSTRUCTIONS

1. Have fishmonger shuck clams. Or carefully shuck clams yourself. Reserve clam juice. Chop clams, if desired, and add to reserved clam juice. Set aside in refrigerator.

2. Heat medium pot over medium-high heat. Chop bacon and add to hot pot. Sauté until crisp, about 5 - 7 minutes. Stir occasionally.

3. Peel and roughly chop onion. Peel garlic. Add to food processor and pulse until finely chopped, about 1 minute. Or mince. Chop parsnips.

4. Drain bacon on paper towels. Set aside. Reserve bacon fat in hot pot.

5. Add onion, garlic, tapioca salt and pepper to hot oiled pot. Sauté until fragrant, about 2 minutes.

6. Add parsnips. Stir in coconut milk and 2 - 3 cups clam juice. Reduce heat to low and simmer for 20 minutes.

7. Remove clams in their juice from refrigerator and add to pot. Stir in remaining clam juice, if desired. Bring to simmer, then cook another 5 minutes.

8. Transfer to serving dishes. Chop parsley and sprinkle over dish with chopped bacon.

9. Serve immediately.

Calamari with Ginger Sauce

Prep Time: 15 minutes

Cook Time: 20 minutes

Servings: 4

INGREDIENTS

12 oz (3/4) medium whole squid (calamari)

2 cage-free eggs

1/4 cup almond flour

1/4 cup coconut flour

1/4 cup arrowroot powder

1/4 teaspoon Celtic sea salt

Water

Ginger Sauce

1 yellow onion

2 inch piece fresh ginger

1 lemon

1/2 cup coconut vinegar (or apple cider vinegar)

1/2 cup pure fish sauce (or tamari or coconut aminos)

1/2 cup tamari (or coconut aminos or liquid aminos)

INSTRUCTIONS

1. For *Ginger Sauce*, peel and chop ginger and onion. Add to food
   processor or high-speed blender and process until coarsely ground,

about 1 minute. Add lemon juice, vinegar, fish sauce and tamari. Process until smooth, about 1 minute.

2. Pour mixture into small pot and heat over medium heat. Bring to simmer. Reduce heat to medium-low and cook until *Ginger Sauce* is reduced and thickened, about 10 - 15 minutes. Stir occasionally. Remove from heat and set aside. Then transfer to serving dish.

3. Have fishmonger clean squid. Or remove innards, clean and rinse squid yourself. Then cut into 1/3 inch rings, keeping tentacles intact.

4. Heat medium pan over medium-high heat. Coat pan with about 1/2 inch coconut oil.

5. Add arrowroot to shallow dish. Blend almond flour, coconut, flour and salt to separate shallow dish. Beat eggs and 1 tablespoon water in small mixing bowl or third shallow dish.

6. Dredge calamari rings and tentacles in arrowroot, shaking off excess. Transfer to dish for storage between steps.

7. Dip dusted squid into egg mixture, tossing gently to coat. Shake off excess and place back on dish.

8. Dredge dipped squid in flour mixture and carefully place directly into hot oil. Do not return to dish. Fry about 3 - 5 minutes, until golden brown and just cooked through. Tentacles cook slightly faster than rings. Turn half way through cooking with chopsticks or tongs.

9. Drain calamari on paper towel, then transfer to serving dish.

10. Serve hot with *Ginger Sauce*.

Thai Steamed Mussels

Prep Time: 10 minutes

Cook Time: 10

Servings: 2

INGREDIENTS

2.5 lbs fresh mussels

1/2 can (about 6.5 oz) coconut milk

3 tablespoons dry white wine (or tamari or coconut vinegar)

2 teaspoons Thai red curry paste

1/2 tablespoon pure fish sauce

1/2 tablespoon raw honey (or agave)

2 garlic cloves

1 bunch fresh cilantro

2 limes

INSTRUCTIONS

1. Have fishmonger clean mussels. Or scrub mussels and remove the beards with pliers yourself, if necessary.

2. Juice limes into large pot with lid. Peel and mince garlic. Add to pot with coconut milk, wine, curry paste, fish sauce and honey. Heat over high heat and bring to boil. Stir frequently.

3. Simmer for 1 minute, then add mussels. Cover with lid and cook until mussels open, about 5 - 8 minutes. Sir occasionally.

4. Remove from heat. Chop cilantro and toss with mussels.

5. Transfer mussels and liquid to serving dish. Serve hot.

Chinese Mustard Baked Salmon

Prep Time: 5 minutes

Cook Time: 20 minutes

Servings: 2

INGREDIENTS

2 (8 oz) salmon fillets (deboned, skin-on)

2 cups bok choy or Chinese broccoli (roughly chopped)

1/2 teaspoon sesame seeds

Parchment paper

Kitchen twine

Mustard Sauce

1/4 cup pure fish sauce

2 tablespoons Chinese hot mustard (or Dijon or spicy brown mustard)

1 tablespoon raw honey (or agave)

1 tablespoon tamari (or coconut aminos)

1 tablespoon coconut oil

1/2 lime

1 garlic clove

1/2 inch piece fresh ginger

INSTRUCTIONS

1. Preheat oven to 400 degrees F. Place large sheet pan on bottom rack of oven. Prepare large sheet of parchment.

2. For *Mustard Sauce*, peel and mince garlic and ginger. Add to small mixing bowl with fish sauce, mustard, honey, tamari, coconut oil and lime juice. Mix to combine. Set aside.

3. Chop bok choy or Chinese broccoli and place in the middle of parchment sheet.

4. Place salmon fillets skin-side down over veggies. Brush well with *Mustard Sauce*. Transfer remaining mustard sauce to serving dish.

5. Gather edges of parchment up over salmon and tie tightly with kitchen twine to form sealed pouch.

6. Place pouch directly on hot baking sheet in hot oven. Bake for 20 minutes.

7. Remove from oven and carefully open pouch to release steam. Transfer veggies and salmon to serving dish.

8. Serve hot with remaining *Mustard Sauce*.

Baked Tilapia Filets

Prep time: 10 minutes

Cook time: 15 minutes

Serves: 4

INGREDIENTS

4 filets of tilapia

¼ tsp chipotle chili pepper powder

1 lemon

1 cup coconut milk

1 clove garlic

1 tsp lemon juice

2 tbsp dill

¼ tsp black ground pepper

INSTRUCTIONS

1. Preheat oven to 350 degrees. Chop the garlic and the dill and cut the lemon into slices.
2. Season tilapia with chipotle chili pepper powder and black ground pepper. Bake for 15 minutes or until tilapia flakes with a fork.
3. Combine coconut milk, garlic, lemon juice and dill in a bowl.
4. Remove fish from oven and pour sauce over the top, placing a lemon wedge over each. Serve immediately or chill 20 minutes and then serve.

Fresh Sashimi Bento Bowl

Prep Time: 20 minutes*

Servings: 1

INGREDIENTS

2 fresh sea scallops (sushi grade)

2 oz fresh salmon filet (sushi grade)

2 oz fresh tuna filet (sushi grade)

1/2 small cucumber

1/2 avocado

1 sheet nori (dried seaweed/sushi paper)

1/2 lemon

1 oz pickled ginger (or 2 inch piece fresh ginger + 2 tablespoons raw apple cider vinegar and 1 tablespoons raw honey)

1 teaspoon real wasabi (or 2 tablespoons fresh ground horseradish)

1/2 teaspoon raw sesame seeds

2 tablespoons salmon roe or caviar (optional)

Sashimi Sauce

2 teaspoons raw sesame oil (or coconut, walnut, almond oil, etc.)

2 teaspoons coconut aminos (or tamari)

1 - 2 teaspoons raw honey

1/2 small scallion

1/2 piece ginger root

INSTRUCTIONS

1. *For fresh pickled ginger, peel ginger and use mandolin, vegetable peeler or slicing attachment on food processor to thinly slice. Add to glass container with vinegar and honey and refrigerate 1 - 7 days.

2. Have fish monger clean and filet tuna and salmon, and remove skin.

3. Place salmon, tuna and scallops in freezer for about 15 minutes to firm.

4. For sashimi sauce, peel ginger and mince. Slice scallion. Add to small mixing bowl with oil, coconut aminos and honey. Transfer to small serving bowl and set aside.

5. Use spiralizer, mandolin or vegetable peeler to thinly slice cucumber, and arrange around serving dish. Cut avocado in half and slice pitted half in peel. Scoop flesh onto serving dish beside fish.

6. Place pickled ginger and wasabi or horse around serving dish.

7. Slice lemon and cut nori into thin strips. Place around serving dish. Place salmon roe or caviar around serving dish (optional).

8. Remove fish from freezer and thinly slice. Arrange fish in center of serving dish. Serve immediately.

Fresh Clams with Cocktail Sauce

Prep Time: 5 minutes*

Servings: 1

INGREDIENTS

12 large little neck clams

3/4 lemon

Raw Cocktail Sauce

1 large tomato

Juice of 1/4 lemon

2 tablespoons raw sesame seeds(or 1 tablespoon raw tahini)

1 tablespoon fresh ground horseradish

Pinch Celtic sea salt

Pinch cracked black pepper

INSTRUCTIONS

1. Have fishmonger shuck clams. *Or carefully shuck clams yourself.

2. Arrange clams around serving dish.

3. Add sesame seeds to food processor or high-speed blender and process until smooth, if using.

4. Or seed tomato and add to processor or blender with tahini, lemon juice, horseradish, salt and pepper. Process until smooth and transfer to small serving bowl.

5. Serving clams with *Raw Cocktail Sauce* immediately.

Asian Shrimp Lettuce Wraps

Prep Time: 35 minutes

Servings: 2

INGREDIENTS

4 large lettuce leaves (thin, flexible ribs)

1 cup cabbage (shredded)

1 small carrot

1/2 green onion

1/2 inch piece fresh ginger

1 small garlic clove

1/2 teaspoon raw sesame seeds

1/2 teaspoon coconut aminos (or tamari or raw apple cider vinegar)

1 teaspoon raw oil (sesame, coconut, walnut, almond, etc.)

Shrimp

10 - 12 medium shrimp

3/4 cup lemon juice (about 5 lemons)

1 teaspoon red pepper flakes

1/2 green onion (scallion)

Almond Sauce

2 tablespoons raw oil (sesame, coconut, walnut, almond, etc.)

1/4 cup raw almond butter (or 1/2 cup raw almonds)

1 tablespoon lemon juice (or coconut aminos or tamari)

1 tablespoons sweetener*

1/2 small mild chili pepper

Water

INSTRUCTIONS

1. For *Shrimp*, slice green onion and reserve half in small mixing bowl. Peel, devein and remove tails from shrimp. Add to separate bowl with lemon juice, remaining green onion and red pepper. Mix to combine. Shrimp should be completely covered in lemon juice. Place in refrigerator for 30 minutes, or until shrimp are opaque.

2. Peel ginger and garlic, and finely grate or mince. Add to green onion with coconut aminos and oil. Mix to combine. Set aside.

3. For *Almond Sauce*, add oil, almond butter or almonds, lemon juice, sweetener and chili pepper to food processor or high-speed blender. Process until smooth and creamy, about 1 - 2 minutes. Add enough water to reach desired consistency. Transfer to serving dish.

4. Shred cabbage and carrot and add to ginger mixture. Toss to coat.

5. Rinse, dry and plate lettuce leaves. Drain shrimp and layer onto lettuce. Top with cabbage mixture and sprinkle on sesame seeds. Roll up lettuce wraps and serve with *Almond Sauce*.

*stevia, raw honey or dried dates

Smoked Salmon Avocado Salad

Prep Time: 10 minutes

Servings: 1

INGREDIENTS

Salad

2 cups soft lettuce leaves (looseleaf or butterhead varieties)

1/2 cup watercress or dandelion leaves (optional)

2 oz smoked salmon

1/2 avocado

1 sprig fresh dill

1 tablespoon caviar (optional)

Avocado Cream Dressing

1/2 avocado

1 sprig fresh dill

1 tablespoon lemon juice

1/2 teaspoon ground black pepper

1/2 teaspoon Celtic sea salt

1/2 coconut

Water

INSTRUCTIONS

1. For *Salad*, rinse, dry and plate lettuce and watercress or dandelion leaves (optional). Cut avocado in half and remover pit. Dice or

slice avocado flesh in peel, then scoop onto greens. Lay smoked salmon over greens.

2. For *Avocado Cream Dressing*, remove coconut flesh from peel and add to food processor or high-speed blender with enough water to reach desired consistency. Process until smooth and creamy, about 1 - 2 minutes. Strain mixture through nut milk bag and place back into blender.

3. Scoop remaining avocado flesh into blender. Add lemon juice, 1 sprig dill, salt and pepper and process until well combined and smooth, about 1 minute.

4. Drizzle *Avocado Cream Dressing* over salad. Mince remaining dill and sprinkle over salad. Dollop caviar over salad (optional).

5. Serve immediately.

stevia, raw honey or dried dates

Tuna Tartar with Avocado and Mango

Prep Time: 15 minutes

Servings: 2

INGREDIENTS

8 oz tuna steak (sushi grade)

1 mango

1 avocado

1 lime

1 garlic clove

Small bunch fresh cilantro

2 tablespoons raw oil (sesame, coconut, almond, walnut, etc.)

1 teaspoon coconut aminos (or raw apple cider vinegar)

1/4 teaspoon red pepper flake

1/4 teaspoon Celtic sea salt

1/4 teaspoon ground pepper

2 tablespoons raw macadamia nuts (optional)

INSTRUCTIONS

1. Add oil, coconut aminos and red pepper flake in small bowl. Cut lime in half and add squeeze of lime. Mix to combine and set aside.

2. Cut avocado in half and remove pit. Dice flesh in peel and scoop into small mixing bowl. Finely chop cilantro. Add to medium mixing bowl with squeeze of remaining lime, salt and pepper. Mix to combine, then set aside.

3. Peel garlic and mince. Cut mango in half around pit. Peel and dice. Add to separate mixing bowl with 1 tablespoon oil and pepper mixture. Toss to coat. Set aside.
4. Dice tuna, discarding any tough white gristle. Finely chop macadamia nuts.
5. Transfer tuna to serving dish. Place in ring mold to form, if preferred. Top with mango and avocado mixtures. Sprinkle on chopped nuts. Drizzle on remaining oil and pepper mixture if preferred.
6. Serve immediately. Or refrigerate 20 minutes and serve chilled.

City Clam Chowder

Prep Time: 35 minutes

Servings: 2

INGREDIENTS

2 dozen live littleneck clams

1 - 1 1/2 cups lemon juice (about 8 lemons)

2 cups tomato juice (about 4 large tomatoes)

2 plum tomatoes

1 celery stalk

1 carrot

1 red bell pepper

1 green bell pepper

1/4 teaspoon cayenne pepper

1/2 teaspoon onion powder

1 teaspoon dried oregano

1 teaspoon dried basil

1 teaspoon ground black pepper

1 teaspoon Celtic sea salt

INSTRUCTIONS

1. Have fishmonger shuck clams. Or carefully shuck clams yourself. Reserve clam juice.
2. Juice lemons into medium mixing bowl. Add clams and toss to coat. Clams should be completely covered in lemon juice. Place in refrigerator for 30 minutes, or until clams are opaque.

3. Juice large tomatoes in juicer then add to food processor or high-speed blender. Or add to food processor or high-speed blender and process, then strain and return to processor.

4. Remove stems, seeds and veins from bell peppers. Cut red and green bell pepper in half. Cut carrot and celery stalks in half. Add half of each veggie to tomato juice with salt and spices. Process until smooth, about 2 minutes. Add to medium mixing bowl. Set aside.

5. Dice plum tomatoes, and remaining celery, carrot, and bell pepper. Add to tomato purée with reserved clam juice, salt and spices.

6. Remove clams from refrigerator and drain lemon juice. Gently rinse, if desired. Add to bowl and mix to combine.

7. Transfer to serving dish and serve immediately.

Salmon Tartar Stack

Prep Time: 10 minutes*

Servings: 2

INGREDIENTS

8 oz boneless, skinless salmon fillet (sushi grade)

2 limes

1 avocado

1 shallot

1 tablespoon raw oil (coconut, walnut, almond, sesame, etc.)

1 teaspoon mustard seeds (or ground mustard)

Medium sprig fresh dill

Celtic sea salt, to taste

Ground black pepper, to taste

2 teaspoons caviar (optional)

INSTRUCTIONS

1. Have fishmonger prepare salmon fillets. Or fillet salmon and remove pin bones and skin.
2. Dice salmon and transfer to serving dish. Top with squeeze of 1/2 lime and sprinkle of salt and pepper. Place in mold to form, if preferred.
3. Peel and thinly slice shallot, then add to small mixing bowl. Juice whole lime into food processor or high-speed blender. Add oil, mustard seeds and pinch of salt and pepper. Process to combine, then add to shallots.

4. Or add lime juice, oil, ground mustard, salt and pepper to shallots. Mix to combine and set aside.

5. Cut avocado in half and remove pit. Dice flesh in peel and scoop into separate mixing bowl. Finely chop dill and add to avocado with squeeze of remaining 1/2 lime, salt and pepper. Mix to combine.

6. Add avocado dill mixture to salmon. Then top with shallot mixture and caviar (optional). Serve immediately.

7. *Or refrigerate 2 hours and serve chilled.

Garlic and White Wine Steamed Mussels

Prep Time: 10 minutes

Cook Time: 5 minutes

Servings: 6

INGREDIENTS

24 fresh green lipped mussels

3 large garlic cloves

1/4 cup ghee (or coconut oil)

1/2 cup white wine (or sparkling apple cider)

1/2 teaspoon sea salt

Medium bunch fresh parsley

INSTRUCTIONS

1. Have fishmonger clean mussels, or scrub mussels and remove the beards with pliers, if necessary.

2. Heat large pan over medium heat. Add ghee or coconut oil and salt.

3. Peel and mince garlic. Add to hot oiled pan and sauté garlic for a few seconds, until aromatic.

4. Add mussels and wine. Cover and cook 3 - 4 minutes, just until most of the mussels open.

5. Remove pan from heat and discard mussels that do not open. Finely chop fresh parsley and add to pan. Toss to combine.

6. Use tongs or slotted spoon to transfer cooked mussels to somewhat deep serving bowl. Pour cooking liquid over mussels.

Shrimp Stuffed Squid

Prep Time: 15 minutes

Cook Time: 25 minutes

Servings: 4

INGREDIENTS

Stuffed Squid

12 medium whole squid (calamari)

8 oz medium shrimp

2 cups baby spinach

1/3 cup almond flour

1 egg

1 tablespoon apple cider vinegar

3 garlic cloves

Small bunch fresh oregano

1/4 teaspoon crushed red pepper flakes

3/4 teaspoon sea salt

2 tablespoons coconut oil

8 wooden toothpicks

Sauce

16 oz (2 cans) organic tomato sauce

1 small onion

2 garlic cloves

1/2 cup dry white wine (or 1/3 cup sparkling apple cider + 3 tablespoons apple cider vinegar)

INSTRUCTIONS

1. Have fishmonger clean squid and peel and devein shrimp. Or clean and rinse squid and peel and devein shrimp yourself.
2. Heat medium pan over medium heat. Add coconut oil to pan.
3. Peel garlic and add to food processor or high-speed blender with shrimp and 4 squid. Pulse until coarse paste forms.
4. Add shrimp paste to medium mixing bowl. Roughly chop spinach and oregano leaves and add to bowl with egg, almond flour, vinegar, red pepper and salt. Mix to combine.
5. Stuff remaining squid bodies with stuffing. Secure closed with toothpicks.
6. Use tongs to add stuffed and secured squid to hot oiled pan. Sear for about 1 minute, then flip.
7. Peel and roughly chop onion and garlic. Add to food processor or high-speed blender with white wine. Process until onion and garlic are well broken down.
8. Pour mixture over seared squid. Add tomato sauce and gently stir to blend. Cover and simmer squid in sauce for 15 minutes.
9. Turn over stuffed squid and continue cooking uncovered another 10 minutes.
10. Remove pan from heat. Remove squid from pan and remove toothpicks from squid with tongs or forks.
11. Transfer squid to serving dish and pour sauce over.
12. Serve hot.

Lobster Newburg

Prep Time: 15 minutes

Cook Time: 25 minutes

Servings: 6

INGREDIENTS

2 (1 lb) live lobsters

2 egg yolks

1/2 cup coconut cream (or kefir + 2 tablespoons sweetener*)

1/4 cup ghee (or cacao butter)

2 tablespoons dry sherry (or 1 tablespoon apple cider vinegar + 1 teaspoon sweetener*)

1/2 teaspoon sea salt

1/4 teaspoon cayenne pepper

1 /4 teaspoon ground nutmeg

Biscuits

1 1/4 cups almond flour

1 egg

2 tablespoons coconut oil

3/4 teaspoon baking soda

1/8 teaspoon ground white pepper

1/4 teaspoon sea salt

INSTRUCTIONS

1. Preheat oven to 350 degrees F. Line sheet pan with parchment paper. Place 4 ceramic ramekins on parchment, and lightly coat bottom with coconut oil.

2. Bring large pot of salted water to boil. Use tongs to carefully place each lobster in boiling water for just 1 minute. Remove from pot. Crack lobster claws and tails and remove meat. Roughly chop, and set aside.

3. For *Biscuits*, separate egg white into medium bowl, and add yolk to small bowl with coconut oil.

4. Beat egg whites to soft peaks with hand mixer or whisk. Mix yolk and oil, almond flour, baking soda, salt and pepper into egg white to form soft, solid dough.

5. Roll dough into eight balls, then flatten into 1/2-inch thick round biscuits with hands. They should fit ramekins snuggly. Place 1 biscuit at bottom of each ramekin. Set remaining biscuits aside on parchment sheet next to ramekins.

6. In small bowl, whisk together egg yolks and coconut cream until well blended.

7. Melt ghee in medium pan over low heat. Stir in egg mixture and sherry. Stir and cook until mixture thickens slightly, about 5 minutes.

8. Add salt, cayenne and nutmeg. Add par cooked lobster meat and cook about 1 minute then remove from heat.

9. Scoop portion of lobster mixture into each ramekin, over biscuit. Top with remaining biscuit.

10. Place sheet pan in oven and bake 15 minutes, until biscuit is golden and firm on top.

11. Remove from oven and let cool slightly.

12. Serve warm.

raw honey or agave nectar

Seafood Paella

Prep Time: 10 minutes

Cook Time: 25 minutes

Servings: 4

INGREDIENTS

1 large head cauliflower

8 oz chorizo (or other smoked sausage)

8 oz large shrimp

12 live little neck clams

12 live mussels

4 bone-in chicken thighs

1 cup chicken stock (or seafood stock)

1 small white onion

2 tablespoons smoked paprika

1 teaspoon saffron

Pinch ground black pepper

Pinch sea salt

2 tablespoons coconut oil

INSTRUCTIONS

1. Heat large pan over medium heat and add coconut oil.
2. Peel and chop onion. Add to hot oiled pan and sauté until translucent, about 2 minutes.
3. Add chicken thighs and brown about 5 minutes. Turn chicken over and cook another 5 minutes.

4. Rinse and clean clams and mussels, and remove any beards with pliers. Peel and devein shrimp. Cut chorizo into 1 inch slices. Set aside.

5. Roughly chop cauliflower and add to food processor with shredding attachment, process to "rice." Or mince cauliflower with knife.

6. Add riced or minced cauliflower to chicken and sauté 2 minutes. Add chorizo, clams, mussels and shrimp. Add paprika and saffron and sauté another 2 minutes.

7. Add chicken or seafood stock and stir to combine. Increase heat to high and bring to simmer. Reduce heat to medium-high and cover. Let simmer about 5 - 7 minutes, until liquid evaporates, shrimp is opaque, and mussels and clams open. Discard any that do not open.

8. Plate and serve hot.

Easy Tuna Tartar Crêpes

Prep Time: 5 minutes

Cook Time: 15 minutes

Servings: 4

INGREDIENTS

Crêpes

1 cup tapioca flour

1 cup coconut milk (not full-fat)

1 egg

1/4 teaspoon sea salt

Coconut oil (for cooking)

Tuna Tartar

12 oz tuna steak (sushi grade)

1/4 teaspoon ground white pepper (or ground black pepper)

1/4 teaspoon sea salt

4 tablespoons caviar

Avocado Cream

1 ripe avocado

1/4 cup full-fat coconut oil

2 tablespoons coconut oil

1/4 lemon

INSTRUCTIONS

1. Heat large non-stick pan over medium heat. Coat evenly with coconut oil.

2. For *Crêpes*, blend all ingredients thoroughly in medium bowl with whisk or hand mixer on low speed.

3. When pan is hot, use ladle or dry measure cup to pour in 1/3 cup of crêpe batter while tilting pan in all directions to evenly spread batter.

4. Cook crêpe about 2 minutes, then carefully flip and cook another 1 - 2 minutes.

5. When both sides are lightly browned, transfer crêpe to plate and re-oil pan. Wait until oil is hot to repeat, until remaining batter is cooked.

6. For *Tuna Tartar*, dice tuna and discard any tough white gristle. Add to bowl with salt and pepper. Gently toss with soft spatula or large spoon. Set aside.

7. For *Avocado Cream*, cut avocado in half and remove pit. Scoop flesh into food processor or high-speed blender. Add coconut milk, coconut oil and squeeze of lemon juice. Process until smooth. Add coconut milk or lemon juice to thin to drizzling consistency, if necessary.

8. Add two tablespoons *Avocado Cream* to *Tuna Tartar* and gently toss to coat.

9. Fill crêpes with *Tuna Tartar* down center and fold over each side. Plate fold-side down and drizzle on remaining *Avocado Cream*, to taste. Dollop caviar onto **Crêpes**.

10. Serve immediately.

Smoked Salmon Eggs Benedict

Prep Time: 15 minutes

Cook Time: 25 minutes

Servings: 4

INGREDIENTS

4 cage free eggs

6 oz smoked salmon

2 sprigs fresh dill

English Muffins

1/3 cup coconut flour

1/3 cup almond flour

2 eggs

1/4 cup almond milk (or low-fat coconut milk)

2 tablespoons coconut oil

1/2 teaspoon baking soda

1 teaspoon apple cider vinegar

Hollandaise Sauce

1/2 cup ghee or coconut oil (melted)

2 egg yolks

1/2 lemon

1/4 teaspoon sea salt

INSTRUCTIONS

1. Preheat oven to 400 degrees F. Coat 2 mini-round cake pans or 4-inch diameter ceramic ramekins with coconut oil. Bring medium pot to simmer with 1 teaspoon salt and 1 teaspoon apple cider vinegar.

2. For *English Muffins*, mix baking soda and apple cider vinegar In small bowl. Set aside and allow to froth.

3. In medium mixing bowl, beat egg whites with hand mixer or whisk until thick and frothy. Add yolks, almond and coconut flour, nut milk, and coconut oil. Mix gently.

4. Add baking soda and vinegar mixture to bowl and blend well until smooth and free of clumps.

5. Pour batter into pans or ramekins and place on sheet pan. Place in oven and bake 15 -18 minutes, until golden brown and center is firm to the touch.

6. Crack eggs into 4 separate small bowls. Coat or spray metal ladle with coconut oil. Hold ladle over simmering water and pour 1 egg into coated ladle. Slowly tilt edge of ladle into hot water, filling it gently while keeping ladle just submerged in water. Do not let egg float out of ladle or submerge ladle into water entirely. Hold and cook egg about 1 - 2 minutes, until whites are opaque and yolk is warmed but still runny. Place poached egg on paper towel to drain. Repeat with remaining eggs.

7. Remove muffins from oven. Loosen from sides of cake pans or ramekins with knife and turn out onto wire rack to cool.

8. For *Hollandaise Sauce*, add egg yolks, squeeze of lemon, and salt to food processor or high-speed blender. Processor for 30 seconds. While processor or blender is running, drizzle in melted ghee or

coconut oil very slowly. Process until all fat is added and emulsified and sauce thickens a bit, about 2 minutes.

9. Cut slightly cool *English Muffins* in half and transfer to serving dish.

10. Layer *English Muffin* halves with smoked salmon, then top with a poached egg. Pour *Hollandaise Sauce* over poached eggs, to taste. Sprinkle with pinch of salt and cracked black pepper, if preferred. Chop dill and sprinkle over eggs.

11. Serve immediately.

All-Natural Seared Tuna Salad

Prep Time: 10 minutes

Cook Time: 10 minutes

Servings: 1

INGREDIENTS

1 cup spinach

1 cup arugula

1 avocado

Seared Tuna

6 oz sushi-grade tuna steak

1 tablespoon sesame oil (or coconut oil)

Juice of 1/2 lemon

1 glove garlic

1/2 inch piece fresh ginger

1 teaspoon sesame seeds

Ginger Glaze

1/2 cup pure fish sauce (or coconut aminos)

1/4 cup apple cider vinegar

Juice of 1 1/2 lemons

2 tablespoons sweetener*

1 inch piece fresh ginger

1 green onion

INSTRUCTIONS

1. For *Ginger Glaze*, peel and grate fresh ginger and slice scallion. Add to small pot with fish sauce, vinegar, sweetener and lemon juice. Heat over medium heat and bring to a simmer. Simmer 5 - 7 minutes, until slightly reduced and thickened. Stir occasionally. Once reduced, transfer to serving dish and refrigerate.

2. For *Seared Tuna*, peel and grate or mince ginger and garlic. Add to small dish with lemon juice and sesame oil and mix to combine. Roll tuna steak in marinade to coat and let sit in dish for 10 minutes in refrigerator.

3. Slice avocado in half and pit. Slice flesh in peel. Place halves together to keep avocado from browning while continuing.

4. Heat small skillet over medium-high heat. Add 1 tablespoon coconut oil.

5. Place marinated tuna in hot oiled pan and sear on each side about 1 minute, until outer flesh is just crisped but inside *is not* cooked through. About 5 minutes.

6. Remove tuna and sprinkle with sesame seeds. Cut tuna into slices.

7. Plate spinach and arugula. Fan out avocado slices over salad.

8. Top salad with *Seared Tuna*. Drizzle on chilled *Ginger Glaze* and serve immediately.

*stevia, raw honey or agave nectar

Tilapia Ceviche

Prep Time: 25 minutes

Servings: 4

INGREDIENTS

1 lb fresh, wild caught skinless tilapia fillets

Juice of 4 limes

Juice of 1 lemon

1 plum tomato

1/2 cucumber

1/2 small red onion

Medium bunch cilantro leaves

1/2 teaspoon sea salt

1/2 teaspoon ground black pepper

1 avocado

1 jalapeño pepper (optional)

INSTRUCTIONS

1. Dice fish with sharp knife. Freeze for 20 minutes to make cutting easier and cleaner, if preferred.
2. Add fish to medium mixing bowl. Juice all limes and 1/2 lemon over fish. Gently mix to combine. Cover and chill in refrigerator for 15 to 20 minutes, until fish is opaque.
3. Drain off liquid from fish and discard. Set fish aside.
4. Seed and dice tomato. Peel and dice cucumber and onion. Stem, seed and vein jalapeño pepper, then mince. Finely chop cilantro.

5. Add everything to marinated fish with salt and pepper. Juice remaining 1/2 lemon and mix to combine.
6. Slice avocado in half and pit and slice flesh.
7. Serve *Tilapia Ceviche* immediately with sliced avocado. Or refrigerate for 20 minutes and serve chilled.

Oyster Po' Boy

Prep Time: 15 minutes

Cook Time: 20 minutes

Servings: 2

INGREDIENTS

Long Rolls

12 oysters

1/2 cup coconut flour

1 egg

1 avocado

1 tablespoon lemon juice

1 sprig fresh dill

1 rib lettuce

1 small tomato

8 - 12 dill pickle chips

1/2 teaspoon black pepper

1/2 teaspoon salt

Coconut oil (for cooking)

INSTRUCTIONS

1. Preheat oven to 350 degrees F. Line sheet pan with parchment paper, or lightly coat with coconut oil. Or lightly coat 6 mini loaf pans with coconut oil.
2. Prepare *Long Rolls* and place in oven.

3. Heat small pan over medium heat. Coat with coconut oil.

4. Add coconut flour to small bowl. Beat egg with salt and pepper in separate mixing bowl. Dip each oyster in beaten egg, then dredge in coconut flour.

5. Place each oyster in hot oiled pan and cook until crispy and lightly browned, about 2 minutes on each side.

6. Remove oysters from pan and drain on paper towels.

7. Finely mince dill. Slice and pit avocado. Scoop flesh into small bowl and mix with lemon juice and dill until smooth. Shred lettuce and slice tomatoes.

8. Remove *Long Rolls* from oven and let cool about 2 minutes.

9. Slice rolls along side and spread with avocado mixture. Place shredded lettuce on bottom of bun, then add 6 fried oysters. Top with tomato slices and pickles.

10. Serve immediately.

Long Rolls

Prep Time: 5 minutes

Cook Time: 15 minutes

Servings: 6

INGREDIENTS

1/4 cup almond flour

1/4 cup coconut flour

1/4 cup full-fat coconut milk

3 eggs

2 tablespoons unsweetened applesauce

2 tablespoons tapioca flour (or arrowroot powder)

1 teaspoon baking powder

1/2 teaspoon sea salt

INSTRUCTIONS

1. Preheat oven to 350 degrees F. Line sheet pan with parchment paper, or lightly coat with coconut oil. Or lightly coat 6 mini loaf pans with coconut oil.

2. Beat eggs, coconut milk and applesauce in medium mixing bowl with hand mixer or whisk.

3. In large mixing bowl, sift together coconut flour, almond flour, tapioca or arrowroot, baking powder and salt. Pour egg mixture into flour mixture and mix until combined.

4. Scoop thick batter onto prepared sheet pan in six long forms. Or pour into six prepared mini loaf pans for uniformity. Smooth batter with knife or spatula.
5. Place in oven and bake for 12 - 15 minutes, or until golden and tops are firm to the touch.
6. Remove from oven and let cool at least 5 minutes.
7. Slice in half or split through top, and serve with your favorite link or filling.

Tuna Sandwich

Prep Time: 10 minutes

Cook Time: 15 minutes

Servings: 1

INSTRUCTIONS

Sandwich Bread

7 oz (1 can) chunk light tuna

1/2 avocado

1/2 small red onion

1 small carrot

1 small celery stalk

1/2 small cucumber

1/2 lemon

1/2 teaspoon paprika

1/4 teaspoon cracked black pepper (or ground black pepper)

1/4 teaspoon sea salt

DIRECTIONS

1. Preheat oven to 350 degrees F. Lightly coat 6 mini round cake pans or medium loaf pan with coconut oil. Bring medium pot of lightly salted water to a boil.

2. Prepare *Sandwich Bread* and place in oven.

3. While bread bakes, drain tuna and add to small mixing bowl. Cut celery stalk and carrot in half length-wise. Peel onion and cucumber. Finely dice celery, carrot and onion. Add to bowl.

4. Slice avocado in half and scoop flesh of non-pit half into bowl. Preserve pitted half in airtight container with pit intact for freshness.

5. Add salt, pepper paprika and squeeze of 1/2 lemon into bowl. Mash together with fork until combined and smooth. Slice cucumber into 1/4 inch rounds.

6. Refrigerate tuna mixture if preferred.

7. Remove *Sandwich Bread* from oven and let cool about 5 minutes.

8. Slice bread and fill with tuna mixture. Top with cucumber slices.

9. Serve immediately.

Sandwich Bread

Prep Time: 5 minutes

Cook Time: 15 minutes

Servings: 6

INGREDIENTS

2 cups almond flour

4 eggs

1/2 cup coconut cream (or melted cacao butter)

1/2 cup arrowroot powder (or tapioca flour)

1/3 cup ground chia seed (or flax meal)

1/4 cup coconut oil

2 tablespoons unsweetened applesauce

1 teaspoon apple cider vinegar

1 teaspoon baking soda

1/2 teaspoon sea salt

INSTRUCTIONS

1. Preheat oven to 350 degrees F. Lightly coat 6 mini round cake pans with coconut oil.
2. Beat eggs, coconut oil, coconut cream, applesauce and vinegar in medium mixing bowl with hand mixer or whisk.
3. In large mixing bowl, sift together almond flour, arrowroot, chia meal, baking soda and salt. Pour egg mixture into flour mixture and mix until well combined.

4. Pour batter into prepared mini cake pans and bake for about 15 minutes, or until golden brown and toothpick inserted comes out clean.

5. Remove from oven and let cool at least 5 minutes.

6. Slice in half and serve with your favorite deli meats or sandwich salads.

NOTE: Lightly oil medium loaf pan and bake for about 25 minutes for **Sandwich Bread** loaf.

Healthy Shrimp Taco

Prep Time: 15 minutes

Cook Time: 20 minutes

Servings: 4

INGREDIENTS

Grain-Free Tortillas

Filling

12 oz medium shrimp

1/2 small red onion

1 fresh jalapeño or (2 oz pickled jalapeño)

1 garlic clove

1/2 inch piece ginger root

1/4 head cabbage (1 cup shredded)

Large bunch cilantro

1 avocado

1 tomato

2 limes

Coconut oil (for cooking)

INSTRUCTIONS

1. Heat large pan over medium-high heat and lightly coat with coconut oil.
2. Prepare *Grain-Free Tortillas*, with 4 smaller portions.

3. Keep tortillas warm and moist in oven set to WARM under damp paper towel.
4. Use clean paper towel to carefully wipe out pan. Add 1 tablespoon coconut oil to pan.
5. Peel and devein shrimp, and remove tail. Peel and mince garlic and ginger. Peel and thinly slice onion. Slice fresh jalapeños.
6. Add shrimp to pan with garlic, ginger, onion and jalapeños. Sauté about 2 minutes, then squeeze juice of 1 lime and sprinkle pinch of salt and pepper over shrimp.
7. Sauté shrimp until just cooked, about 5 minutes. Remove from heat.
8. Grate radish, shred cabbage, dice tomato. Slice avocado in half, remove pit, and slice flesh in peel. Chop cilantro.
9. Remove tortillas from oven and layer with sautéed shrimp and onions. Top with shredded cabbage, radish, tomato and avocado slices. Finish with large pinch of cilantro and squeeze of lime.
10. Fold tortillas and serve warm.

Grain-Free Tortillas

Prep Time: 5 minutes

Cook Time: 10 minutes

Servings: 2

INGREDIENTS

2 tablespoons almond flour

2 tablespoons coconut flour

1/2 tablespoon flax meal (or ground chia seed)

2 eggs

1/4 cup water (plus extra)

2 tablespoons coconut oil

1/4 teaspoon baking powder

Coconut oil (for cooking)

INSTRUCTIONS

1. Heat medium frying pan over medium-high heat and coat with coconut oil.

2. Whisk together eggs, coconut oil and 1/4 cup water in medium bowl.

3. In separate mixing bowl, blend coconut flour, almond flour, flax or chia seed, and baking powder.

4. Slowly whisk as you pour flour mixture into wet ingredients. If batter appears too thick to spread fairly thin in pan, add up to 4 tablespoon water 1 tablespoon at a time.

5. Use ladle or dry measure cup to pour 1/2 of batter into hot oiled pan. Tilt pan in circular motion as you pour so batter spreads thinly.
6. Cook batter for about 2 minutes or until slightly golden and firm. Flip tortilla with tongs or spatula and cook another 2 minutes. Remove and place on paper towel or parchment.
7. Cook remaining batter for 2 minutes on each side. Re-oil pan as necessary.
8. Fill warm tortillas with meat or veggies of choice and serve warm.

Coconut Shrimp

Prep Time: 10 minutes

Cook Time: 15 minutes

Servings: 4

INGREDIENTS

3 egg whites

1 lb large shrimp

1 cup flaked coconut

1/2 teaspoon garlic powder

1/2 teaspoon ground white pepper (or ground black pepper)

1 teaspoon sea salt

Coconut oil (for cooking)

Mango Salsa

1 ripe mango

1/2 small white onion

1 small jalapeño

Juice of half lime

INSTRUCTIONS

1. Preheat oven to 425 degrees F. Line sheet pan with parchment paper. Or place oven-safe wire rack over sheet pan.
2. Add coconut to shallow dish.
3. Beat egg whites with salt, pepper and garlic powder in a large mixing bowl with hand mixer or whisk until light and fluffy.

4. Peel and devein shrimp. Leave tails on. Add shrimp to egg whites to coat.

5. Let excess egg white drain from shrimp, then add to coconut flakes. Toss to coat. Return shrimp to egg whites, then coconut flakes again. Press shrimp into coconut and coat well.

6. Place the shrimp on prepared sheet pan. Brush lightly with liquid coconut oil.

7. Place in oven and bake for 5 - 7 minutes. Then turn shrimp over, brush with coconut oil, and bake another 5 - 7 minutes, until coconut is golden brown and shrimp are bright pink.

8. For *Mango Salsa*, slice mango around pit. Peel and dice flesh. Peel and dice onion. Mince jalapeño, discarding seeds and stem. Add to small serving dish juice of half a lime. Mix to combine.

9. Remove shrimp from oven and allow to cool for a few minutes.

10. Serve warm with *Mango Salsa*.

Clams Casino

Prep Time: 5 minutes

Cook Time: 25 minutes

Servings: 4

INGREDIENTS

18 medium littleneck clams

1/3 cup dry white wine (or 1/4 cup sparkling apple cider + 2 tablespoons apple cider vinegar)

4 - 6 slices nitrate-free bacon

1 large red bell pepper

4 shallots

2 large garlic cloves

1/3 cup almonds

1/4 teaspoon dried oregano

1/4 teaspoon ground black pepper

1/4 teaspoon sea salt

2 tablespoons coconut oil

INSTRUCTIONS

1. Have fishmonger shuck clams and loosen meat from bottom shell. Reserve bottom shell.
2. Heat large pan over medium-high heat and add coconut oil. Line sheet pan with parchment or aluminum foil.

3. Finely chop bacon and add to hot pan. Sauté until crisp, about 5 minutes. Use slotted spoon to remove cooked bacon from pan and drain on paper towel. Set aside.

4. Preheat oven to 500 degrees F.

5. Remove seeds, stem and veins from bell pepper, then finely chop. Peel and finely chop shallots. Peel and mince garlic. Add to hot bacon drippings with oregano, salt and pepper. Sauté about 5 minutes, until shallots are tender and translucent.

6. Add wine to pan and simmer until just evaporated, about 2 minutes. Remove pan from heat and stir in reserved bacon.

7. Arrange clams in bottom shells on prepared sheet pan. Spoon bacon mixture onto the clams, packing slightly into mound.

8. Finely chop almonds, or add to food processor or high-speed blender and pulse until finely chopped, with some texture remaining. Sprinkle chopped almonds over clams.

9. Place in oven and bake about 10 minutes, until clams are just cooked through and topping is golden brown and aromatic.

10. Remove from oven and transfer to serving dish.

11. Serve immediately.

Crispy Soft Shell Crab With Garlic Lemon Aioli

Prep Time: 10 minutes

Cook Time: 10 minutes

Servings: 2

INGREDIENTS

2 soft shell crabs

1/4 cup almond flour

2 tablespoons tapioca flour

1 teaspoon paprika

1/4 teaspoon dried oregano

1/4 teaspoon dried thyme

1/4 teaspoon onion powder

1/2 teaspoon garlic powder

1/2 teaspoon black pepper

1/2 teaspoon sea salt

Pinch cayenne pepper (optional)

Coconut oil

Garlic Lemon Aioli

1 garlic clove

1 egg yolk

1/2 lemon

1/8 teaspoon sea salt

1/4 - 2/3 cup coconut oil

INSTRUCTIONS

1. Have fishmonger clean soft-shell crabs. Or clean crabs yourself, then rinse.

2. Heat medium pan over medium-high heat. Coat with coconut oil.

3. Combine almond and tapioca flours with spices in shallow dish. Dredge crabs in seasoned flour mixture.pat flour onto crabs and gently shake off excess.

4. Place coated crabs in hot oiled pan belly-side down. Cook about 5 minutes, until golden and crisp, then flip. Add coconut oil if necessary and cook another 5 minutes, until golden and cooked through. Transfer to paper towel and drain.

5. For *Garlic Lemon Aioli*, peel garlic and add to food processor or high-speed blender with egg yolk, juice of 1/2 lemon and sea salt while crabs cook. Process until garlic is finely ground.

6. Slowly drizzle in enough coconut oil to bring mixture together while running processor. Process until mixture emulsifies and thicken slightly. Transfer to serving dish.

7. Transfer cooked crabs to serving dish and serve immediately with aioli.

Almond Crusted Pan Seared Scallops

Prep Time: 15 minutes

Cook Time:10 minutes

Servings: 2

INGREDIENTS

12 large sea scallops (shelled and cleaned)

1/2 cup organic white wine (or sparkling apple cider)

1/3 cup raw almonds

1 tablespoon ground coriander

1/4 teaspoon fresh ground nutmeg

1/4 teaspoon black pepper

1/2 teaspoon sea Salt

1/2 tablespoon coconut oil

INSTRUCTIONS

1. Preheat oven to 375 degrees F.
2. Add scallops, wine and 1/4 teaspoon salt to small mixing bowl. Set aside to marinate for 10 minutes.
3. Place almonds on dry baking sheet and place in oven. Toast 7 - 8 minutes.
4. Heat medium pan over medium-high heat and add coconut oil.
5. Remove almonds from oven and add to food processor with coriander, nutmeg, 1/4 teaspoon salt and black pepper. Pulse to grind coarsely.

6. Add almond coating to shallow dish. Remove scallops from marinade and coat each side in almond mixture.
7. Place coated scallop in hot oiled pan and grill 2 - 3 minutes on each side.
8. Remove scallops and serve immediately with your favorite greens and vinaigrette.

Basque Style Cod Fish Stew

Prep Time: 30 minutes*

Cook Time: 45 minutes

Servings: 4

INGREDIENTS

8 oz (1/2 lb) salted cod fish

1/2 cup tomato sauce

1/4 cup white wine (or 3 tablespoons white grape juice + 1 tablespoon apple cider vinegar)

2 cage-free eggs

2 large parsnips

1 onion (yellow, red or white)

1 large garlic clove

1/4 cup golden raisins

2 oz roasted red bell peppers (jarred)

2 tablespoons green olives (pitted)

1 teaspoon capers

1 bay leaf

1/4 cup coconut oil

Water

INSTRUCTIONS

1. *Soak salted cod in 2 quarts of water for 8 hours. Change water 3 times throughout soaking time. Drain and cut fish into chunks.

2. Bring small pot of salted water to boil. Hard boil eggs about 10 minutes. Drain and set aside in cold water to cool. Crack and peel shells.
3. Peel onion and garlic. Mince garlic. Slice onion, parsnips, and cooled eggs.
4. In order, layer half of parsnips, cod, onion, eggs, capers, garlic, olives, peppers and raisins in medium pot. Add bay leaf, then half of tomato sauce and coconut oil.
5. In order, layer remaining parsnips, cod, onion, eggs, capers, garlic, olives, peppers and raisins. Add 1 cup water and wine on top. Do not stir.
6. Heat pot over medium heat, cover and bring to a boil. Reduce heat to medium-low and simmer until parsnips are tender, about 30 minutes.
7. Transfer to sourcing dishes and serve immediately.

All-Natural Lobster Bisque

Prep Time: 25 minutes

Cook Time: 40 minutes

Servings: 4

INGREDIENTS

16 oz (1 lb) lobster meat (claws and tail from 2 - 3 lobsters)

4 cups vegetable broth

1 can (13.5 oz) full-fat coconut milk (or lite coconut milk)

1 can (6 oz) organic tomato paste

2 tablespoons coconut aminos (apple cider vinegar or liquid aminos)

2 leeks

2 carrots

2 celery stalks

4 large garlic cloves

2 bay leaves

1/2 teaspoon dried basil

1/2 teaspoon dried thyme

1 teaspoon dried oregano

1 teaspoon fresh cracked black pepper (or ground black pepper)

Celtic sea salt, to taste

1 small bunch freash parsley (for garnish)

2 tablespoons ghee (or bacon fat, cacao butter, or coconut oil)

INSTRUCTIONS

1. Chop leeks, carrots and celery. Peel garlic and chop. Add to medium pot with vegetable broth, oregano, basil, thyme, pepper and salt to taste. Add tomato paste and stir to combine. Simmer about 25 minutes.

2. Bring large pot salted water to boil. Boil each lobster about 2 minutes. Let cool, then crack shells and remove meat from claws and tail. Roughly chop and set aside.

3. Pour veggies and broth into food processor or high-speed blender. Process until puréed, about 2 minutes.

4. Add puréed mixture back to pot and heat over medium heat. Bring to simmer and add chopped lobster meat. Stir to combine. Simmer until lobster is cooked through and tender, about 10 minutes.

5. Transfer to serving dish and serve hot.

Red Snapper Soup

Prep Time: 30 minutes

Cook Time: 1 hour

Servings: 4

INGREDIENTS

1 (2 1/2 lbs) whole red snapper (gutted, scaled and cleaned)

2 small onions (yellow, white or red)

3 tomatoes

2 large carrots

4 celery stalks (with leaves)

4 large parsnips

1 medium zucchini cut part-way through, lengthwise

1 lemon

Celtic sea salt, to taste

1/4 cup coconut oil

Water

INSTRUCTIONS

1. Have fishmonger gut, scale and clean fish.
2. Peel and thinly slice onions. Roughly chop carrot, celery and parsnips.
3. Add to large pot with 4 cups water and coconut oil. Bring to a boil over medium heat. Cover and simmer for 15 minutes.

4. Roughly chop tomatoes and zucchini and add to pot. Cover and boil simmer for 20 minutes. Add fish to pot and cover. Simmer for about 25 minutes.
5. Remove from heat. Remove fish and 1/4 veggies from pot and set aside. Squeeze juice of lemon over reserved fish and veggies.
6. Pour remaining veggies and liquid into food processor or high-speed blender. Process until puréed, about 2 minutes.
7. Cut fish into portions. Transfer reserved fish and veggies to serving dish.
8. Pour puréed soup over fish and veggies and serve hot.

Vegetarian Cookbook

Table of Contents

Spicy Kale Quiche

Eggplant with Pesto Topping

Spicy Zucchini Eggplant Dine

Lettuce Nut Salad

Eggplant with Red Sauce

Sweet Potatoes Roast

Quick 'n' Easy Pepper Quiche

"Green Bean" Casserole

Mushroom Masala

Easy Matzo Ball Soup

Butternut Squash Soup

Mexican Tomato Soup

Creamy "Cheesy" Broccoli Soup

Pita Bites

Simple Gazpacho + Tortilla Chips

Grain-Free Tortillas

Healthy Veggie Burger

Soft Burger Buns

Egg Salad Sandwich

Sandwich Bread

Kelp Noodle Salad

Zucchini Salad with Sundried Tomato Sauce

Quick Raw Avocado Slaw

Vegetarian Texas Chili

All-Natural Caesar Salad

Spiced Walnut Autumn Salad

Pecan Apricot Spinach Salad

Southern Style Egg Salad

Pesto Tomato Caprese

Cashew Crunch Kelp Noodle Salad

Dill Stuffed Tomatoes

Squash Blossom Stuffers

Indian Egg Fried Rice

Spicy Kale Quiche

Prep time: 10 minutes

Cook time: 15 minutes

Serves: 4

INGREDIENTS

8 cage-free eggs

2 tbsp extra virgin olive oil

1 7oz bag of Kale greens

1 shallot

¼ tsp chipotle chili pepper powder

2 cloves garlic

½ lemon

2 tbsp coconut oil

¼ tbsp ground black pepper

INSTRUCTIONS

1. Place a steamer basket in the bottom of a large pot and fill with water; if you see water rise above the bottom of the basket, pour some out. Bring the water to a boil.
2. Wash the kale and remove the stems. Mince the garlic and shallot and squeeze the juice from the lemon into a bowl.
3. In a large pan, add the eggs and extra virgin olive oil. Mixing in the chipotle chili pepper powder, scramble the eggs, breaking them up until they form many small pieces, tender yet firm.
4. Place the kale in the pot and steam until tender and bright-green.

5. Remove the kale from the pot and combine with the eggs. Add the garlic, shallot and lemon juice, drizzle the coconut oil over top and add the ground black pepper. Mix and stir thoroughly.
6. Serve immediately or chill 20 minutes and then serve.

Eggplant with Pesto Topping

Prep time: 10 minutes

Cook time: 8 minutes

Serves: 4

INGREDIENTS

1 large, thick eggplant

6-8 tomatoes

4 tbsp olive oil

¼ cup fresh basil

2 cloves garlic

INSTRUCTIONS

1. Preheat the grill. Slice the eggplant lengthwise into ½" thick slices, or ensuring that you have 4 slices. Slice the tomatoes into ¼" thick slices. Combine 4 tbsp olive oil with basil and garlic in a food processor and puree together.

2. Grill the eggplant until browned, turning once, about 3-4 minutes per side.

3. Remove eggplant from the grill and lay the tomato slices out over each piece. Top with the pesto puree and serve.

Spicy Zucchini Eggplant Dine

Prep time: 15 minutes

Cook time: 20 minutes

Serves: 4

INGREDIENTS

3 small zucchini

1 eggplant

2 green peppers

6 tomatoes

1 onion

2 medium carrots

1 four-inch sweet orange pepper

1 cup water

1 tbsp extra virgin olive oil

INSTRUCTIONS

1. Using a julienne peeler, peel zucchini, eggplant and green peppers. Green peppers may be too tough for a julienne peeler, in which case try to simulate the effect of one using a knife. Combine the above in a pan with extra virgin olive oil and saute over medium heat, stirring, for 5 minutes.

2. Meanwhile, cut tomatoes into quarters, carrots into ½" thick slices, dice sweet pepper and dice onion. In a saucepan, combine the above with water and cook over medium heat until carrot is tender,

about 15 minutes. Once finished, blend using an immersion blender, or pour into a blender and puree.

3. Pour the sauce over the zucchini, eggplant and peppers and serve.

Lettuce Nut Salad

Prep time: 10 min

Cook time: 6-8 minutes

Serves: 4

INGREDIENTS

1 7oz bag of Romaine lettuce

1 cup strawberries

1 cup blueberries

1 cup kiwi

½ cup almonds

½ cup walnuts

2 cups coconut milk

1 tbsp arrowroot

1 tsp cinnamon

¼ tsp chipotle chili pepper powder

INSTRUCTIONS
1. Dice the fruits. In a saucepan, combine coconut milk, arrowroot, cinnamon and chipotle chili pepper powder over medium heat. Cook, stirring, for 4 minutes. Add the walnuts and almonds to the sauce and continue cooking until slightly thick.
2. Combine lettuce and fruit in a bowl and drizzle the sauce over the top. Serve immediately or chill 20 minutes and then serve.

Eggplant with Red Sauce

Prep time: 10 minutes

Cook time: 8 minutes

Serves: 2

INGREDIENTS

½ large eggplant cut lengthwise

4 asparagus stalks

2 cloves garlic

1 yellow tomato

2 tsp fresh cilantro

2 tbsp extra virgin olive oil

1 cup organic red sauce

INSTRUCTIONS

1. In a medium saucepan, heat the red sauce on low and keep hot.
2. Slice the eggplant into ½ inch slices, 8 slices total. Heat 1 ½ extra virgin olive oil in a frying pan on medium heat. Cook the eggplant two minutes on one side and another two minutes on the other side. Transfer to a plate.
3. Add ½ tbsp to the pan. Slice the garlic. Rinse the asparagus and cut each asparagus stalk into 3 equal lengths.
4. Add garlic and asparagus to pan and sautee until asparagus is tender.
5. Dice yellow tomato and cilantro and mix together.

6. Place four slices of eggplant on each plate. Spoon red sauce over each slice. Cover with tomato/cilantro mixture and evenly distribute asparagus and garlic cloves.
7. Serve.

Sweet Potatoes Roast

Prep time: 10 minutes

Cook time: 30 minutes

INGREDIENTS

3 sweet potatoes

¼ cup extra virgin olive oil

¼ tsp Celtic sea salt

¼ tsp smoked paprika

INSTRUCTIONS

1. Preheat oven to 500 degrees.
2. Peel the potatoes and cut them into small wedges. In a large bowl, combine potato wedges, extra virgin olive oil, Celtic sea salt and smoked paprika. Mix well until all wedges are coated in all ingredients.
3. Place on a baking sheet and bake for 30 minutes, turning once halfway through, and continue cooking until they are well browned.
4. Remove from oven and let cool. Serve.

Quick 'n' Easy Pepper Quiche

Prep time: 5 minutes

Cook time: 3-6 minutes

INGREDIENTS

2 cage-free eggs

1 small onion

1 clove garlic

½ red bell pepper

1 tbsp extra virgin olive oil

¼ tsp smoked paprika

¼ tsp ground black pepper

INSTRUCTIONS
1. Finely chop onion, garlic and red bell pepper.
2. Pour extra virgin olive oil into a pan over medium heat.
3. Crack eggs and pour into a small bowl. Combine with onion, garlic and red bell pepper and whisk until mixed together.
4. Pour contents of bowl into pan and add smoked paprika and ground black pepper. Scramble until desired doneness.
5. Serve.

"Green Bean" Casserole

Prep Time: 5 minutes

Cook Time: 20 minutes

Servings: 12

INGREDIENTS

Casserole

4 cups asparagus

2 cups button mushrooms

1 cup nut milk

1/2 cup cegetable stock

2 tablespoons tapioca flour

1 teaspoon ground white pepper (or ground black pepper)

1 teaspoon garlic powder

1 teaspoon onion powder

Crispy Onions

1/2 cup almond meal

1/2 medium onion (yellow or white)

1 cage-free egg

1 teaspoon paprika

1 teaspoon onion powder

1/4 teaspoon ground black pepper

1 teaspoon Celtic sea salt

Coconut oil (for cooking)

INSTRUCTIONS

1. Preheat oven to 350 degrees F. Bring medium pot of water plus 1/2 teaspoon salt to a boil.

2. For *Casserole*, cut asparagus stalks into quarters. Add to boiling water for about 3 - 4 minutes, until tender but not mushy. Drain and shock in ice bath to stop cooking an preserve color. Set aside.

3. Add tapioca flour and vegetable stock to large pan and heat over medium-high heat. Whisk until smooth, then add nut milk, white pepper, garlic and onion powder.

4. Slice mushrooms and add to pan. Stir and thicken about 8 minutes, until thick and creamy.

5. Add asparagus to pan and stir to coat. Pour into baking or casserole dish and bake about 20 minutes, until heated through. Remove from oven and let cool BOUT 5 minutes.

6. Heat medium pan on medium-high heat and coat with coconut oil.

7. For *Crispy Onions*, whisk egg in medium bowl. In shallow dish, mix almond meal with spices.

8. Peel and slice onion. Toss onions in beaten egg, then in seasoned almond meal to coat. Add to hot oiled pan and fry until crispy and golden brown, about 1 - 2 minutes.

9. Drain *Crispy Onions* on paper towel, then sprinkle over *Casserole*. Serve warm.

Mushroom Masala

Prep Time: 10 minutes

Cook Time: 25 minutes

Servings: 8

INGREDIENTS

1 head cauliflower

1 1/2 cups tomato purée (or tomato sauce)

1 pint (2 cups) mushrooms

1 onion

1 chili pepper

1 /2 green bell pepper

1 large garlic clove

1 inch piece fresh ginger

2 teaspoons coriander leaves (optional)

1 teaspoon garam masala

1/2 teaspoon cayenne pepper

1/2 teaspoon ground coriander

1/2 teaspoon Celtic sea salt

3 tablespoons coconut oil or ghee

INSTRUCTIONS

1. Roughly chop cauliflower, then rice cauliflower in food processor, or mince. Add to medium pot with enough water to cover. Heat pot over medium heat and cook until just tender, about 8 minutes. Drain and transfer to serving dish.

2. Heat medium pan over medium heat. Add oil or butter to hot pan.

3. Peel and finely dice onions. Remove seeds, veins and stem from bell pepper and dice. Slice chili pepper. Peel and mince garlic and onion. Add to hot oiled pan and sauté about 5 minutes.

4. Slice mushrooms and add to pan with tomato, salt and spices. Finely chop coriander leaves and add to pan (optional). Sauté and let simmer about 10 - 12 minutes, stirring occasionally.

5. Transfer to serving dish and serve hot with cauliflower rice.

Easy Matzo Ball Soup

Prep Time: 5 minutes*

Cook Time: 10 minutes

Servings: 6

INGREDIENTS

6 cups vegetable stock

2 cups almond flour

4 cage-free egg yolks

1/4 teaspoon ground white pepper (or ground black pepper)

2 teaspoons Celtic sea salt

INSTRUCTIONS

1. In a medium bowl, beat eggs,1 teaspoon salt and pepper until light and frothy, about 2 minutes. Sift almond flour into bowl and mix until dough comes together.
2. *Cover dough with parchment, if preferred, and refrigerate 2 - 4 hours.
3. Add 1 teaspoon salt to large pot of water and bring to boil. Add vegetable stock to medium pot and heat over medium heat.
4. Remove dough from refrigerator and roll into balls. Carefully place dough balls in boiling water. Reduce heat to low, cover and simmer 20 minutes, until cooked through.
5. Transfer matzo balls to serving dish with slotted spoon. Ladle heated vegetable stock over matzo balls and serve hot.

Butternut Squash Soup

Prep Time: 10 minutes

Cook Time: 1 hour

Servings: 4

INGREDIENTS

1 medium-large butternut squash (about 2 cups diced)

2 cups veggie stock

1/2 cup coconut milk (optional)

1/2 onion (white, yellow or sweet)

1/2 large carrot

1/2 celery stalk

1/2 teaspoon ground coriander (optional)

1 cinnamon stick

Ground black pepper, to taste

Celtic sea salt, to taste

2 tablespoons shelled pumpkin seeds (toasted or raw)

2 tablespoons ghee (or coconut oil)

2 tablespoons coconut oil

INSTRUCTIONS

1. Heat oven to 375 degrees F. Heat medium cast iron pan over medium-high heat. Add butter to hot oiled pan.
2. Peel squash and remove seeds. Dice and add to hot oiled pan with salt and pepper, to taste. Sauté until golden, about 3 - 4 minutes.

Place pan in oven and roast until browned on all sides, about 15 minutes.

3. Heat medium pot over medium-low heat. Add coconut oil to hot pot.

4. Peel and dice onion, celery and carrot. Add to hot oiled pot with cinnamon stick, salt and pepper to taste. Sauté until soft but not browned, about 10 minutes.

5. Remove squash from oven and let cool slightly. Add food processor or high-speed blender and process until puréed.

6. Add vegetable broth and coriander (optional) to pot. Increase heat to medium and bring to boil. Simmer about 5 minutes.

7. Stir in squash purée and simmer about 10 minutes. Discard cinnamon stick.

8. Add mixture to food processor or high-speed blender and purée until smooth. Or blend with immerse or stick blender until smooth.

9. Transfer mixture back to hot pot and stir in coconut milk (optional). Transfer to serving dish.

10. Sprinkle with pumpkin seeds and cracked black pepper. Serve hot.

Mexican Tomato Soup

Prep Time: 10 minutes

Cook Time: 40 minutes

Servings: 4

INGREDIENTS

2 cans (14.5 oz) organic crushed tomatoes

2 cans (11.5) organic tomato juice

5 large tomatoes (or 10 plum tomatoes)

1/2 cup coconut milk

1 red bell pepper (or 1/4 cup roasted red peppers, jarred)

1/4 red onion (or yellow or white onion)

2 garlic cloves

1/2 Serrano chili pepper (or other chili pepper) (optional)

1 tablespoon tapioca flour (or arrowroot powder)

2 tablespoons fresh Mexican oregano (or 1 teaspoon dried oregano)

2 large basil leaves

1 teaspoon fresh cracked black pepper (or ground black pepper)

Celtic sea salt, to taste

1 small bunch cilantro (for garnish)

2 tablespoons ghee (or cacao butter, or coconut oil)

INSTRUCTIONS

    1. Juice tomatoes and set aside.

2. Roast red bell pepper over stove burner or until broiler, if using. Turn to char on all sides until skins sears. Rub off blackened skin. Cut in half and remove seeds, stem and veins.

3. Heat medium pot over medium-high heat. Add fat to hot pot.

4. Peel onion and garlic. Dice onion, roasted and red pepper. Mince garlic and Serrano pepper (optional). Add to hot oiled pot and sauté until fragrant, about 2 minutes.

5. Add tapioca and coconut milk. Stir to combine. Let cook about 2 minutes.

6. Chiffon (thinly slice) basil. Add to pot with tomato juice, crushed tomatoes, oregano, pepper and salt, to taste. Stir to combine.

7. Bring to simmer, then reduce heat to low. Simmer and reduce about 30 minutes, or until desired consistency is reached.

8. Transfer to serving dish. Chop cilantro and sprinkle over dish for garnish.

9. Serve hot.

Creamy "Cheesy" Broccoli Soup

Prep Time: 10 minutes

Cook Time: 30 minutes

Servings: 4

INGREDIENTS

1 large head broccoli

2 cups vegetable broth

1 cup nut milk

1/2 cup nutritional yeast

1 medium onion (white or yellow)

2 garlic cloves

1 tablespoon coconut aminos (or liquid aminos or tamari)

1 tablespoon mustard powder

Celtic sea salt, to taste.

1 teaspoon ground white pepper (or 1/2 teaspoon ground black pepper)

2 tablespoons bacon fat (or coconut oil, cacao butterr ghee)

Water

INSTRUCTIONS

1. Heat medium pot over medium heat. Add fat or oil to hot pot.
2. Peel onion and garlic. Chop and add to hot pot. Sauté until fragrant, about 2 minutes.
3. Chop broccoli and add to pot with vegetable broth. Increase heat and bring to boil. Cover and boil about 15 - 20 minutes until broccoli is softened.

4. Pour pot in to food processor or high-speed blender with nutritional yeast, coconut aminos, spices and salt, to taste. Process until smooth, about 1 - 2 minutes. Add enough water to reach desired consistency.

5. Transfer to serving dish and serve immediately.

6. Or add back to pot and heat through over medium heat. Then serve.

Pita Bites

Prep Time: *5 minutes

Cook Time: 20 minutes

Servings: 1

INGREDIENTS

Pita Bites

1 cup tapioca flour/starch

1 teaspoon ground chia seed (or flax meal)

1 egg

2 tablespoons coconut oil

1/4 cup water

1/2 teaspoon baking soda

1/4 teaspoon sea salt

Almond Hummus

1 cup skinless almonds

1/3 cup tahini

1 garlic clove

Juice of 1/2 lemon

Zest of 1/2 lemon

1/4 teaspoon sea salt

1/4 cup water

2 tablespoons pine nuts

INSTRUCTIONS

1. *Soak almonds overnight in enough water to cover. Drain and rinse.

2. Preheat oven to 375 degrees F. Cover sheet pan with parchment paper or baking mat. Heat small pot over low heat.

3. For *Pita Bites*, mix 1/3 cup tapioca flour with chia meal, water and 1 tablespoon coconut oil in pot. Stir until mixture comes together. Remove from heat and cool in freezer.

4. In medium bowl, blend remaining tapioca flour, baking soda and salt. Then add egg and remaining oil. Mix until combined.

5. Add cooled chia mixture to bowl and mix to combine. Then remove and knead to form dough.

6. Form large round disk, then use rolling pin to flatten on lined baking sheet. Cut out circles with biscuit cutter or drinking glass, or cut triangles with pizza cutter. Re-roll excess dough and repeat until all dough is used.

7. Arrange pita pieces on sheet pan and place in oven. Bake about 10 minutes. Carefully turn over with spatula and bake another 5 - 7 minutes, or until crisp.

8. Remove from oven and let cool completely. Place in lidded container or sealable lunch bag and serve room temperature.

9. For *Almond Hummus*, add 1/2 of water to all ingredients in food processor or bullet blender and process. Add just enough water to smooth blend.

10. Scrape hummus into lidded container and serve chilled or room temperature with *Pita Bites*.

Simple Gazpacho + Tortilla Chips

Prep Time: 20 minutes

Cook Time: 10 minutes

Servings: 4

INGREDIENTS

Grain-Free Tortillas

Gazpacho

2 (11.5 oz) cans organic tomato juice (or 3 cups juiced tomatoes)

4 plum tomatoes

2 red bell peppers

1 red onion

1 cucumber

3 garlic cloves

1/4 cup apple cider vinegar

1/4 cup coconut oil (or 2 tablespoons coconut oil and 2 tablespoons flavorful oil [walnut, almond, sesame, etc.])

1 teaspoon cracked black pepper (or ground black pepper)

1/2 tablespoon sea salt

INSTRUCTIONS

1. Seed cucumber and tomatoes. Seed, stem and vein bell peppers. Peel onion and garlic. Dice veggies, mince garlic, and add to medium serving bowl.

2. Add tomato juice, vinegar, oil, salt and pepper, and mix well. Place in refrigerator.

3. Heat medium pan over medium-high heat and coat with coconut oil.

4. For *Tortilla Chips*, prepare *Grain-Free Tortillas*.

5. Add more coconut oil to hot pan and allow to heat up. Cut tortillas into wedges with pizza cutter or sharp knife.

6. Add tortilla wedges back to hot pan in single layer and cook about 30 seconds on each side, until golden and crisp. Drain on paper towel. Repeat with remaining tortilla wedges.

7. Transfer warm *Tortilla Chips* to serving dish. Serve immediately with chilled *Gazpacho*.

Grain-Free Tortillas

Prep Time: 5 minutes

Cook Time: 10 minutes

Servings: 2

INGREDIENTS

2 tablespoons almond flour

2 tablespoons coconut flour

1/2 tablespoon flax meal (or ground chia seed)

2 eggs

1/4 cup water (plus extra)

2 tablespoons coconut oil

1/4 teaspoon baking powder

Coconut oil (for cooking)

INSTRUCTIONS

1. Heat medium frying pan over medium-high heat and coat with coconut oil.
2. Whisk together eggs, coconut oil and 1/4 cup water in medium bowl.
3. In separate mixing bowl, blend coconut flour, almond flour, flax or chia seed, and baking powder.
4. Slowly whisk as you pour flour mixture into wet ingredients. If batter appears too thick to spread fairly thin in pan, add up to 4 tablespoon water 1 tablespoon at a time.

5. Use ladle or dry measure cup to pour 1/2 of batter into hot oiled pan. Tilt pan in circular motion as you pour so batter spreads thinly.

6. Cook batter for about 2 minutes or until slightly golden and firm. Flip tortilla with tongs or spatula and cook another 2 minutes. Remove and place on paper towel or parchment.

7. Cook remaining batter for 2 minutes on each side. Re-oil pan as necessary.

8. Fill warm tortillas with meat or veggies of choice and serve warm.

Healthy Veggie Burger

Prep Time: 5 minutes

Cook Time: 20 minutes

Servings: 4

INGREDIENTS

Soft Burger Bun

Veggie Burger

2 eggs

1/2 head cauliflower

2 medium carrots

1 small white onion

1 cup walnuts (1/2 cup ground)

1/4 cup almond flour

2 tablespoons tapioca flour

2 tablespoons ground chia seed (or flax meal)

2 cloves garlic

1 teaspoon paprika

1 teaspoon ground black pepper

1 teaspoon sea salt

Topping

1 avocado

1 heirloom tomato

1 white onion

2 ribs romaine lettuce (or preferred lettuce)

INSTRUCTIONS

1. Preheat oven to 350 degrees F. Line sheet pan with parchment paper, or lightly coat with coconut oil. Or lightly coat 6 mini round cake pans with coconut oil.
2. Prepare *Soft Burger Buns* and place in oven.
3. While bread bakes, line dish with parchment paper.
4. Add walnuts and almond four to food processor or bullet blender. Process until finely ground. Add to medium mixing bowl.
5. Peel small onion and garlic. Add to processor or blender with cauliflower and carrots. Process until finely ground. Add eggs, tapioca and chia. Process until mixture becomes thickened and has batter-like consistency.
6. Add veggie mixture and spices to mixing bowl. Mix all ingredients together with hands or wooden spoon until fully combined and uniform.
7. Form veggie mixture into 4 patties and place on parchment lined dish. Place in freezer for 10 minutes.
8. Heat medium skillet over medium-high heat and add 1 tablespoon coconut oil.
9. Peel onion. Make 4 thick slices, keeping full ring intact. Using spatula, place full rings into hot oiled pan. Sear 1 minute on each side. Set aside on paper towel to drain.
10. Reduce heat to medium and coat pan with coconut oil.
11. Remove veggie patties from freezer and place in hot oiled pan. Cook 5 minutes, then carefully flip with spatula and cook another 5 minutes.

12. Remove *Soft Burger Bun* from oven and let cool about 5 minutes.

13. Cut lettuce ribs in half. Cut tomato into 4 thick slices. Slice avocado in half, pit and slice flesh in peel.

14. Slice bun in half and place lettuce on bottom bun, followed by tomato slice. Add burger patty, then grilled onion ring. Finish with a few slices of avocado and top bun.

15. Serve immediately.

Soft Burger Buns

Prep Time: 5 minutes

Cook Time: 15 minutes

Servings: 6

INGREDIENTS

1/4 cup almond flour

1/4 cup coconut flour

4 eggs

2 tablespoons coconut oil

2 tablespoons unsweetened applesauce

1 teaspoon flax meal (or ground chia seed)

1 teaspoon baking powder

1/2 teaspoon sea salt

INSTRUCTIONS

1. Preheat oven to 350 degrees F. Line sheet pan with parchment paper, or lightly coat with coconut oil. Or lightly coat 6 mini round cake pans with coconut oil.

2. Beat eggs, coconut oil and applesauce in medium mixing bowl with hand mixer or whisk.

3. In large mixing bowl, sift together coconut flour, almond flour, flax or chia meal, baking powder and salt. Pour egg mixture into flour mixture and mix until combined.

4. Scoop thick batter onto prepared sheet pan in six 4 inch rounds. Or pour into six prepared mini cake pans for uniformity. Smooth batter with knife or spatula.

5. Place in oven and bake for 12 - 15 minutes, or until tops are firm to the touch and golden.

6. Remove from oven and let cool at least 5 minutes.

7. Slice in half and serve with your favorite patty or filling.

Egg Salad Sandwich

Prep Time: 5 minutes

Cook Time: 15 minutes

Servings: 2

INGREDIENTS

Sandwich Bread

Avocado Egg Salad

8 eggs

1 avocado

1/4 cup dill pickle relish

3 tablespoons organic mustard

2 teaspoons paprika

1/2 teaspoon ground black pepper

1/4 teaspoon sea salt

INSTRUCTIONS

1. Preheat oven to 350 degrees F. Lightly coat 6 mini round cake pans or medium loaf pan with coconut oil. Bring medium pot of lightly salted water to a boil.
2. Prepare *Sandwich Bread* and place in oven.
3. While bread bakes, gently add eggs to hot water with tongs and cook about 8 - 10 minutes.
4. Drain eggs in colander and run under cold water to cool.

5. While eggs cool, slice and pit avocado. Scoop flesh into medium mixing bowl. Add relish, mustard, salt and spices.

6. Crack eggs shells and peel. Add boiled eggs to medium mixing bowl.

7. Using a fork, mash ingredients together until smooth mixture with soft chunks forms.

8. Remove *Sandwich Bread* from oven and let cool about 5 minutes.

9. Slice bread and fill with *Avocado Egg Salad*.

10. Serve immediately. Or refrigerate about 20 minutes and serve chilled.

Sandwich Bread

Prep Time: 5 minutes

Cook Time: 15 minutes

Servings: 6

INGREDIENTS

2 cups almond flour

4 eggs

1/2 cup coconut cream (or melted cacao butter)

1/2 cup arrowroot powder (or tapioca flour)

1/3 cup ground chia seed (or flax meal)

1/4 cup coconut oil

2 tablespoons unsweetened applesauce

1 teaspoon apple cider vinegar

1 teaspoon baking soda

1/2 teaspoon sea salt

INSTRUCTIONS
1. Preheat oven to 350 degrees F. Lightly coat 6 mini round cake pans with coconut oil.
2. Beat eggs, coconut oil, coconut cream, applesauce and vinegar in medium mixing bowl with hand mixer or whisk.
3. In large mixing bowl, sift together almond flour, arrowroot, chia meal, baking soda and salt. Pour egg mixture into flour mixture and mix until well combined.

4. Pour batter into prepared mini cake pans and bake for about 15 minutes, or until golden brown and toothpick inserted comes out clean.
5. Remove from oven and let cool at least 5 minutes.
6. Slice in half and serve with your favorite deli meats or sandwich salads.

NOTE: Lightly oil medium loaf pan and bake for about 25 minutes for **Sandwich Bread** loaf.

Kelp Noodle Salad

Prep Time: 5 minutes

Cook Time: 5 minutes

Servings: 2

INGREDIENTS

1 package (12 oz) kelp noodles

1/2 lemon

1 small cucumber

1 small red bell pepper

1 large carrot

Small bunch cilantro

2 large basil leaves

Orange Avocado Dressing

1 avocado

1 large orange

1/2 lemon

5 large basil leaves

1/4 teaspoon ground black pepper

1/4 teaspoon cayenne pepper or red pepper flake (optional)

Large bunch cilantro

INSTRUCTIONS

1. Rinse and drain kelp noodles. Add to medium bowl and soak 5
   minutes in warm water and juice of 1/2 lemon. Or bring medium

pot of water with juice of 1/2 lemon to a boil and cook kelp noodles for 5 minutes, if softer texture preferred.

2. Peel, seed and cut cucumber in half width-wise. Cut bell pepper in half, then remove stem, seeds and veins. Use vegetable peeler or grater to make long, thin slices of carrot. Thinly slice cucumber and bell pepper lengthwise.

3. Add veggies and drained kelp noodles to medium mixing bowl.

4. For *Orange Avocado Dressing*, add basil and cilantro leaves to food processor or bullet blender with juice of orange and process to break down leaves. Slice avocado in half and remove pit. Scoop flesh into processor with juice of 1/2 lemon, black pepper and hot pepper (optional). Process until thick and until creamy.

5. Pour *Orange Avocado Dressing* over sliced veggies and kelp noodles. Toss to coat.

6. Serve immediately. Or refrigerate for 20 minutes and serve chilled.

Zucchini Salad with Sundried Tomato Sauce

Prep Time: 20 minutes*

Servings: 2

INGREDIENTS

1 medium zucchini

1 tomato

5 sundried tomatoes

1 garlic clove

2 fresh basil leaves

1 tablespoon raw virgin coconut oil (or 2 tablespoons warm water)

1/4 teaspoon ground white pepper (or black pepper)

1/4 teaspoon sea salt

INSTRUCTIONS

1. Run zucchini through spiralizer, slice into long, thin shreds with knife, or use vegetable peeler to make flat, thin slices. Sprinkle with a pinch of salt and pepper, and gently toss to coat.
2. Add tomato, sundried tomatoes, peeled garlic, basil, coconut oil or warm water, and remaining salt and pepper to food processor or bullet blender. Process until sauce of desired consistency forms.
3. Transfer zucchini pasta to serving bowls. Top with tomato sauce and serve immediately.
4. Or refrigerate for 20 minutes and serve chilled.

Quick Raw Avocado Slaw

Prep Time: 10 minutes*

Cook Time: 20 minutes

Servings: 4

INGREDIENTS

1/2 head cabbage (2 cups shredded)

1 avocado

1 carrot

Zest of 1 lemon

Juice of 1 lemon

1 tablespoon raw honey

2 tablespoons apple cider vinegar

1 teaspoon ground white pepper (or black pepper)

1 teaspoon sea salt

INSTRUCTIONS

1. Cut avocado in half and remove pit. Scoop flesh into large mixing bowl and mash with fork.
2. Remove any tough outer leaves and core from cabbage. Shred cabbage and carrot. Add to bowl with vinegar, honey, salt and pepper. Zest *then* juice lemon, and add.
3. Toss to combine.
4. Serve immediately. Or and place in refrigerator for 20 minutes and serve chilled.

Vegetarian Texas Chili

Prep Time: 10 minutes*

Servings: 2

INGREDIENTS

5 - 6 plum tomatoes

1/2 teaspoon dried cumin

1/4 teaspoon chili powder

1/4 teaspoon onion powder

1/4 teaspoon garlic powder

1 teaspoon fresh oregano leaves (or 1/4 teaspoon dried oregano)

1/2 teaspoon ground black pepper

1/4 teaspoon cayenne pepper or red pepper flakes (optional)

1 teaspoon Celtic sea salt

1 teaspoon chia seed (or flax seed)

1/2 cup raw cashews

Water

INSTRUCTIONS

1. *Soak raw cashews in enough water to cover overnight in refrigerator. Drain and rinse. Set aside.

2. Grind chia or flax in food processor or high-speed blender. Set aside.

3. Juice tomatoes. Or add to food processor or high-speed blender and process. Add enough water to reach desired consistency, if necessary. Then strain.

4. Add tomato juice, ground chia or flax, 1/2 of soaked cashews, salt, pepper and spices to blender. Process until smooth, about 1 - 2 minutes.
5. Stir in remaining soaked cashews.
6. Pour into serving bowls and serve immediately.

All-Natural Caesar Salad

Prep Time: 10 minutes

Servings: 1

INGREDIENTS

2 cups chopped romaine lettuce

Almond Parmesan

1/4 cup raw almonds

1 teaspoon raw apple cider vinegar

1 teaspoon nutritional yeast (optional)

1/4 teaspoon garlic powder

1/4 teaspoon onion powder

1/4 teaspoon dried oregano

1/4 teaspoon Celtic sea salt

Caesar Dressing

2 tablespoons raw cashews (or raw sunflower seeds)

2 tablespoons raw sunflower seeds

1 tablespoon raw pine nuts (or raw sesame seeds or raw tahini)

2 tablespoons lemon juice

1 teaspoon sweetener*

1 garlic clove

3/4 teaspoon coconut aminos (or nutritional yeast)

1/2 teaspoon dried dill (optional)

Cracked or ground black pepper, to taste

Water

INSTRUCTIONS

1. Rinse, dry and plate romaine lettuce.
2. For *Almond Parmesan*, add almonds, vinegar, salt, spices and nutritional yeast (optional) to food processor or high-speed blender. Process until almonds are coarsely ground and resemble ground parmesan cheese. Set aside.
3. For *Caesar Dressing*, peel garlic and add to food processor or high-speed blender with sweetener and lemon juice. Process until smooth. Then add remaining ingredients and process until smooth, about 1 - 2 minutes. Add enough water to reach desired consistency.
4. Drizzle *Caesar Dressing* over salad and sprinkle with *Almond Parmesan*. Serve immediately.

* raw honey or dried dates

Spiced Walnut Autumn Salad

Prep Time: 10 minutes

Servings: 1

INGREDIENTS

Salad

2 cups red lettuce leaves (or other colorful lettuce variety)

1/2 cup arugula

1/2 ripe pear

Spiced Walnuts

1/4 cup walnuts (halves or pieces)

1 tablespoons raw honey (or 1 dried date plus 1 tablespoon water)

1/4 teaspoon ground cinnamon

1/8 teaspoon ground ginger

1/4 teaspoon fresh ground nutmeg

1/8 teaspoon vanilla

1/4 teaspoon ground cardamom (optional)

Orange Vinaigrette

1 orange

2 tablespoons raw apple cider vinegar

2 teaspoons sweetener*

1 teaspoon raw walnut oil (or coconut, almond, sesame oil, etc.)

1 teaspoon raw tahini or sesame seeds (optional)

1 teaspoon ground mustard seeds (or whole mustard seeds)

1/4 teaspoon cracked or ground black pepper

INSTRUCTIONS

1. For *Salad*, rinse, dry and plate lettuce and arugula. Slice pear in half, and remove seeds. Top greens with sliced pears.

2. For *Spiced Walnuts*, process date and water in food processor or high-speed blender until smooth and add to small mixing bowl, if using. Or combine walnuts, spices and raw honey in small mixing bowl. Sprinkle over *Salad*.

3. For *Orange Vinaigrette*, zest and juice orange. Add to food processor or high-speed blender with vinegar, sweetener, spices and tahini (optional) and process until smooth, about 1 minute.

4. Drizzle *Orange Vinaigrette* over salad and serve immediately.

*stevia, raw honey or dried dates

Pecan Apricot Spinach Salad

Prep Time: 10 minutes

Servings: 1

INGREDIENTS

Salad

2 cups spinach leaves

1/2 cup chopped kale leaves

4 - 5 dried apricots

3 tablespoons pecans (halves or pieces)

Honey Mustard Vinaigrette

2 tablespoons raw honey (or 2 dried dates + 2 tablespoons water)

2 tablespoons ground mustard (or mustard seed)

2 tablespoons raw apple cider vinegar

3 tablespoons raw oil (coconut, walnut, almond, sesame, etc.)

3/4 teaspoons Celtic sea salt

INSTRUCTIONS

1. For *Salad*, rinse, dry and plate spinach and kale. Chop dried apricots. Sprinkle apricots and pecans over greens.

2. For *Honey Mustard Vinaigrette*, add honey, mustard, vinegar, oil and salt to food processor or high-speed blender and process until smooth, about 1 minute.

3. Drizzle *Honey Mustard Vinaigrette* over salad and serve immediately.

Southern Style Egg Salad

Prep Time: 5 minutes

Cook Time: 15 minutes

Servings: 4

INGREDIENTS

8 cage-free eggs

1 avocado

1 celery stalk

1/4 sweet onion

1/4 cup sweet pickle relish (or dill pickle relish + 1 tablespoon raw honey, agave or date butter)

1/4 cup organic mustard

2 teaspoons paprika

1/2 teaspoon ground black pepper

1/4 teaspoon Celtic sea salt

INSTRUCTIONS

1. Bring medium pot of lightly salted water to a boil. Leave enough room in pot for eggs.
2. Gently add eggs to hot water with tongs and cook about 10 minutes.
3. Drain eggs into colander in sink. Fill pot with cold water and add eggs back to pot. Let cold water run slowly over eggs in pot to cool.

4. Slice and pit avocado. Scoop flesh into medium mixing bowl. Thinly slice celery. Peel and finely dice onion. Add to mixing bowl with relish, mustard, salt and spices. Mix with large spoon to combine.

5. Crack cooled eggs and peel off shells. Add boiled eggs to medium mixing bowl.

6. Use a fork or knife to chop eggs. Use large spoon to mix and mash ingredients together until smooth mixture with soft chunks forms. Stir to combine.

7. Transfer to serving dish and serve immediately. Or refrigerate about 20 minutes and serve chilled.

Pesto Tomato Caprese

Prep Time: 5 minutes

Servings: 2

INGREDIENTS

1 large yellow tomato

1 large red tomato

Small bunch fresh basil

Celtic sea salt, to taste

Crack or ground black pepper, to taste

Basil Pesto

2 cups basil leaves (packed)

1/4 cup raw pine nuts

1/2 - 1/3 cup raw oil (coconut, walnut, almond, sesame, etc.)

2 garlic cloves

1/2 lemon (or 1 tablespoon raw apple cider vinegar)

1/4 teaspoon Celtic sea salt

INSTRUCTIONS

1. For *Basil Pesto*, peel garlic and add to food processor or high-speed blender with squeeze of 1/2 lemon. Process until finely chopped. Add pine nuts, basil, oil and salt and process until finely ground, about 1 minute.

2. Slice tomatoes and plate in alternating colors. Sprinkle with salt and pepper. Chiffon basil leaves.

3. Spread *Basil Pesto* over tomato slices and top with fresh basil. Serve immediately.

Cashew Crunch Kelp Noodle Salad

Prep Time: 10 minutes*

Servings: 2

INGREDIENTS

1 package (12 oz) kelp noodles

1/2 lemon

1/2 small red bell pepper

Cashew Sauce

1 cup raw cashews

1/2 small red bell pepper

1/2 lemon

1 tablespoon coconut aminos (or raw apple cider vinegar)

2 large basil leaves

1/2 teaspoon smoked paprika

1/2 teaspoon ground black pepper

1/2 teaspoon Celtic sea salt

1/4 teaspoon ground turmeric (optional)

1/4 teaspoon smoked chili powder (optional)

Water

INSTRUCTIONS

1. *Soak 3/4 cup cashews in enough water to cover at least 4 hours, or overnight in refrigerator. Drain and rinse.

2. Drain and rinse kelp noodles. Add to medium bowl with warm water and juice of 1/2 lemon. Set aside 5 minutes.

3. Cut bell pepper in half. Remove stem, seeds and veins and set half of pepper aside. Julienne (thinly slice) remaining bell pepper and add to medium mixing bowl.

4. For *Crunchy Cashew Sauce*, add soaked cashews, bell pepper, juice of 1/2 lemon, coconut aminos, basil, salt and spices to food processor or high-speed blender. Process until smooth, about 2 minutes. Add enough water to reach desired consistency. Set aside.

5. Drain kelp noodles and add to sliced bell pepper. Add *Cashew Sauce* and toss to coat. Transfer noodles to serving dishes.

6. Roughly chop remaining 1/4 cup cashews. Sprinkle noodles and serve immediately. Or refrigerate for 20 minutes and serve chilled.

Dill Stuffed Tomatoes

Prep Time: 15 minutes*

Servings: 2

INGREDIENTS

4 medium tomatoes

1 celery stalk

1 small carrot

1 green onion (scallion)

1/3 cup sunflower seeds

1/2 red bell pepper

1/4 small red onion (or sweet onion)

1/2 teaspoon Celtic sea salt

Dill Dressing

1/2 cup raw cashews

1 tablespoon raw apple cider vinegar (or coconut aminos)

1 teaspoon ground mustard (or mustard seeds)

1/2 lemon

1 small garlic clove

2 sprigs fresh dill

1/2 teaspoon Celtic sea salt

1/4 teaspoon ground white pepper (or pinch ground black pepper)

Water

INSTRUCTIONS

1. *Soak cashews in enough water to cover at least 4 hours, or overnight in refrigerator. Drain and rinse.

2. Cut tops off tomatoes and scoop out seeds. Set aside.

3. Finely dice celery and carrot. Slice green onion. Peel and dice onion. Add to medium mixing bowl. Remove stem, seeds and veins from bell pepper, then dice. Add to bowl with sprinkle of salt. Set aside.

4. For *Dill Dressing*, peel garlic and add to food processor or high-speed blender with soaked cashews, vinegar, mustard, squeeze of lemon, dill, salt and pepper. Process until smooth and creamy, about 1 - 2 minutes. Add enough water to reach desired consistency.

5. Pour *Dill Dressing* over chopped veggies. Toss to coat.

6. Plate hollowed tomatoes and stuff with *Dill Dressing* veggie mixture. Serve immediately.

Squash Blossom Stuffers

Prep Time: 10 minutes*

Servings: 4

INGREDIENTS

16 squash blossoms

1/2 cup walnuts

1 avocado

1 small onion

1/2 sprig fresh dill

1/2 lemon

1/2 teaspoon dried thyme

1/2 teaspoon ground white pepper (or ground black pepper)

1/2 teaspoon Celtic sea salt

1 teaspoon dried tarragon (optional)

Water

INSTRUCTIONS

1. *Gently rinse blossoms and pat dry. Let air dry for 30 minutes.

2. Cut avocado in half and remove pit. Scoop flesh into food processor or high-speed blender with walnuts, dill, squeeze of lemon, salt, pepper and spices. Process until smooth, about 2 minutes. Add enough water to reach desired consistency.

3. Peel onion and mince. Add to small mixing bowl with avocado mixture. Mix to combine.

4. Spoon mixture into squash blossoms. Serve immediately.

Indian Egg Fried Rice

Prep Time: 10 minutes

Cook Time: 15 minutes

Servings: 2

INGREDIENTS

1/2 head cauliflower

4 cage-free eggs

1 small carrot

1/2 red bell pepper

1/2 yellow bell pepper

1/4 onion (yellow or white)

2 small green onions (scallions)

2 tablespoons pure fish sauce (or coconut aminos or liquid aminos)

1 tablespoon coconut aminos (or coconut vinegar or liquid aminos)

1 teaspoon raw honey (or date butter or agave)

1 teaspoon sesame oil (optional)

1 large garlic clove

1/2 piece fresh ginger

1/2 teaspoon red pepper flake

Celtic sea salt, to taste

Coconut oil (for cooking)

Water

INSTRUCTIONS

1. Cut cauliflower into florets and add to food processor with shredding attachment to rice. Or finely mince cauliflower. Set aside.
2. Heat medium pan or wok over high heat. Lightly coat with coconut oil.
3. Whisk eggs in medium mixing bowl. Set aside.
4. Remove stems, seeds and veins from bell peppers, then julienne (thinly slice). Finely dice carrot. Slice green onions. Peel and mince garlic, ginger and onion.
5. Add red pepper flakes to hot oiled pan. Sauté until just cooked fragrant, about 30 seconds. Add garlic, ginger and onion and sauté about 1 minute.
6. Add cauliflower to hot pan. Sauté about 5 minutes, until cauliflower is golden and a bit softened.
7. Add carrot, peppers and 1/2 green onions. Cook another 2 - 5 minutes, until cauliflower is cooked through. Add a few tablespoons of water and cover with lid to steam, if desired.
8. Push veggies aside and make well (opening) in center of pan. Pour whisked eggs into well in center and carefully scramble until fully cooked, about 2 minutes. Mix eggs into veggies.
9. Remove from heat and transfer to serving dish. Sprinkle remaining green onions over dish and serve hot.

Made in the USA
San Bernardino, CA
20 December 2014